A London Plane-Tree and Other Verse

A London Plane-Tree and Other Verse

Amy Levy

MINT EDITIONS

A London Plane-Tree and Other Verse was first published in 1889.

This edition published by Mint Editions 2021.

ISBN 9781513295848 | E-ISBN 9781513297347

Published by Mint Editions®

 MINT
EDITIONS

minteditionbooks.com

Publishing Director: Jennifer Newens
Design & Production: Rachel Lopez Metzger
Project Manager: Micaela Clark
Typesetting: Westchester Publishing Services

Contents

Moods and Thoughts

A LONDON PLANE-TREE

A London Plane-Tree

Green is the plane-tree in the square,
 The other trees are brown;
They droop and pine for country air;
 The plane-tree loves the town.

Here from my garret-pane, I mark
 The plane-tree bud and blow,
Shed her recuperative bark,
 And spread her shade below.

Among her branches, in and out,
 The city breezes play;
The dun fog wraps her round about;
 Above, the smoke curls grey.

Others the country take for choice,
 And hold the town in scorn;
But she has listened to the voice
 On city breezes borne.

London in July

What ails my senses thus to cheat?
    What is it ails the place,
That all the people in the street
    Should wear one woman's face?

The London trees are dusty-brown
    Beneath the summer sky;
My love, she dwells in London town,
    Nor leaves it in July.

O various and intricate maze,
    Wide waste of square and street;
Where, missing through unnumbered days,
    We twain at last may meet!

And who cries out on crowd and mart?
    Who prates of stream and sea?
The summer in the city's heart—
    That is enough for me.

A March Day in London

The east wind blows in the street today;
The sky is blue, yet the town looks grey.
'Tis the wind of ice, the wind of fire,
Of cold despair and of hot desire,
Which chills the flesh to aches and pains,
And sends a fever through all the veins.

From end to end, with aimless feet,
All day long have I paced the street.
My limbs are weary, but in my breast
Stirs the goad of a mad unrest.
I would give anything to stay
The little wheel that turns in my brain;
The little wheel that turns all day,
That turns all night with might and main.

What is the thing I fear, and why?
Nay, but the world is all awry—
The wind's in the east, the sun's in the sky
The gas-lamps gleam in a golden line;
The ruby lights of the hansoms shine,
Glance, and flicker like fire-flies bright;
The wind has fallen with the night,
And once again the town seems fair
Thwart the mist that hangs i' the air.

And o'er, at last, my spirit steals
A weary peace; peace that conceals
Within its inner depths the grain
Of hopes that yet shall flower again.

Ballade of an Omnibus

To see my love suffices me.

—*Ballades in Blue China*

Some men to carriages aspire;
On some the costly hansoms wait;
Some seek a fly, on job or hire;
Some mount the trotting steed, elate.
I envy not the rich and great,
A wandering minstrel, poor and free,
I am contented with my fate—
An omnibus suffices me.

In winter days of rain and mire
I find within a corner strait;
The 'busmen know me and my lyre
From Brompton to the Bull-and-Gate.
When summer comes, I mount in state
The topmost summit, whence I see
Crœsus look up, compassionate—
An omnibus suffices me.

I mark, untroubled by desire,
Lucullus' phaeton and its freight.
The scene whereof I cannot tire,
The human tale of love and hate,
The city pageant, early and late
Unfolds itself, rolls by, to be
A pleasure deep and delicate.
An omnibus suffices me.

Princess, your splendour you require,
I, my simplicity; agree
Neither to rate lower nor higher.
An omnibus suffices me.

BALLADE OF A SPECIAL EDITION

He comes; I hear him up the street—
    Bird of ill omen, flapping wide
The pinion of a printed sheet,
    His hoarse note scares the eventide.
Of slaughter, theft, and suicide
    He is the herald and the friend;
Now he vociferates with pride—
    A double murder in Mile End!

A hanging to his soul is sweet;
    His gloating fancy's fain to bide
Where human-freighted vessels meet,
    And misdirected trains collide.
With Shocking Accidents supplied,
    He tramps the town from end to end.
How often have we heard it cried—
    A double murder in Mile End.

War loves he; victory or defeat,
    So there be loss on either side.
His tale of horrors incomplete,
    Imagination's aid is tried.
Since no distinguished man has died,
    And since the Fates, relenting, send
No great catastrophe, he's spied
    This double murder in Mile End.

Fiend, get thee gone! no more repeat
    Those sounds which do mine ears offend.
It is apocryphal, you cheat,
    Your double murder in Mile End.

Straw in the Street

Straw in the street where I pass today
Dulls the sound of the wheels and feet.
'Tis for a failing life they lay
        Straw in the street.

Here, where the pulses of London beat,
Someone strives with the Presence grey;
Ah, is it victory or defeat?

The hurrying people go their way,
Pause and jostle and pass and greet;
For life, for death, are they treading, say,
        Straw in the street?

Between the Showers

Between the showers I went my way,
    The glistening street was bright with flowers;
It seemed that March had turned to May
        Between the showers.

Above the shining roofs and towers
    The blue broke forth athwart the grey;
Birds carolled in their leafless bowers.

Hither and thither, swift and gay,
    The people chased the changeful hours;
And you, you passed and smiled that day,
        Between the showers.

OUT OF TOWN

Out of town the sky was bright and blue,
    Never fog-cloud, lowering, thick, was seen to frown;
Nature dons a garb of gayer hue,
        Out of town.

Spotless lay the snow on field and down,
    Pure and keen the air above it blew;
All wore peace and beauty for a crown.

London sky, marred by smoke, veiled from view,
    London snow, trodden thin, dingy brown,
Whence that strange unrest at thoughts of you
        Out of town?

THE PIANO-ORGAN

My student-lamp is lighted,
    The books and papers are spread;
A sound comes floating upwards,
    Chasing the thoughts from my head.

I open the garret window,
    Let the music in and the moon;
See the woman grin for coppers,
    While the man grinds out the tune.

Grind me a dirge or a requiem,
    Or a funeral-march sad and slow,
But not, O not, that waltz tune
    I heard so long ago.

I stand upright by the window,
    The moonlight streams in wan:—
O God! with its changeless rise and fall
    The tune twirls on and on.

London Poets

(In Memoriam)

They trod the streets and squares where now I tread,
With weary hearts, a little while ago;
When, thin and grey, the melancholy snow
Clung to the leafless branches overhead;
Or when the smoke-veiled sky grew stormy-red
In autumn; with a re-arisen woe
Wrestled, what time the passionate spring winds blow;
And paced scorched stones in summer:—they are dead.

The sorrow of their souls to them did seem
As real as mine to me, as permanent.
Today, it is the shadow of a dream,
The half-forgotten breath of breezes spent.
So shall another soothe his woe supreme—
"No more he comes, who this way came and went."

The Village Garden

To E. M. S.

Here, where your garden fenced about and still is,
    Here, where the unmoved summer air is sweet
With mixed delight of lavender and lilies,
    Dreaming I linger in the noontide heat.

Of many summers are the trees recorders,
    The turf a carpet many summers wove;
Old-fashioned blossoms cluster in the borders,
    Love-in-a-mist and crimson-hearted clove.

All breathes of peace and sunshine in the present,
    All tells of bygone peace and bygone sun,
Of fruitful years accomplished, budding, crescent,
    Of gentle seasons passing one by one.

Fain would I bide, but ever in the distance
    A ceaseless voice is sounding clear and low;—
The city calls me with her old persistence,
    The city calls me—I arise and go.

Of gentler souls this fragrant peace is guerdon;
    For me, the roar and hurry of the town,
Wherein more lightly seems to press the burden
    Of individual life that weighs me down.

I leave your garden to the happier comers
    For whom its silent sweets are anodyne.
Shall I return? Who knows, in other summers
    The peace my spirit longs for may be mine?

LOVE, DREAMS, & DEATH

Ah Love! could you and I with Him conspire
To grasp this sorry Scheme of Things entire,
Would not we shatter it to bits—and then
Re-mould it nearer to the Heart's Desire!

—Omar Khayyám

NEW LOVE, NEW LIFE

I

She, who so long has lain
    Stone-stiff with folded wings,
Within my heart again
    The brown bird wakes and sings.

Brown nightingale, whose strain
    Is heard by day, by night,
She sings of joy and pain,
    Of sorrow and delight.

II

'Tis true,—in other days
    Have I unbarred the door;
He knows the walks and ways—
    Love has been here before.

Love blest and love accurst
    Was here in days long past;
This time is not the first,
    But this time is the last.

Impotens

If I were a woman of old,
    What prayers I would pray for you, dear;
My pitiful tribute behold—
    Not a prayer, but a tear.

The pitiless order of things,
    Whose laws we may change not nor break,
Alone I could face it—it wrings
    My heart for your sake.

Youth and Love

What does youth know of love?
    Little enough, I trow!
He plucks the myrtle for his brow,
    For his forehead the rose.
      Nay, but of love
    It is not youth who knows.

The Dream

Believe me, this was true last night,
Tho' it is false today.

—A. M. F. Robinson

A fair dream to my chamber flew:
Such a crowd of folk that stirred,
Jested, fluttered; only you,
You alone of all that band,
Calm and silent, spake no word.
Only once you neared my place,
And your hand one moment's space
Sought the fingers of my hand;
Your eyes flashed to mine; I knew
All was well between us two.

    *   *   *   *   *

On from dream to dream I past,
But the first sweet vision cast
Mystic radiance o'er the last.

    *   *   *   *   *

When I woke the pale night lay
Still, expectant of the day;
All about the chamber hung
Tender shade of twilight gloom;
The fair dream hovered round me, clung
To my thought like faint perfume:—
Like sweet odours, such as cling
To the void flask, which erst encloses
Attar of rose; or the pale string
Of amber which has lain with roses.

On the Threshold

O God, my dream! I dreamed that you were dead;
Your mother hung above the couch and wept
Whereon you lay all white, and garlanded
With blooms of waxen whiteness. I had crept
Up to your chamber-door, which stood ajar,
And in the doorway watched you from afar,
Nor dared advance to kiss your lips and brow.
I had no part nor lot in you, as now;
Death had not broken between us the old bar;
Nor torn from out my heart the old, cold sense
Of your misprision and my impotence.

The Birch-Tree at Loschwitz

At Loschwitz above the city
    The air is sunny and chill;
The birch-trees and the pine-trees
    Grow thick upon the hill.

Lone and tall, with silver stem,
    A birch-tree stands apart;
The passionate wind of spring-time
    Stirs in its leafy heart.

I lean against the birch-tree,
    My arms around it twine;
It pulses, and leaps, and quivers,
    Like a human heart to mine.

One moment I stand, then sudden
    Let loose mine arms that cling:
O God! the lonely hillside,
    The passionate wind of spring!

In the Night

Cruel? I think there never was a cheating
    More cruel, thro' all the weary days than this!
This is no dream, my heart kept on repeating,
    But sober certainty of waking bliss.

Dreams? O, I know their faces—goodly seeming,
    Vaporous, whirled on many-coloured wings;
I have had dreams before, this is no dreaming,
    But daylight gladness that the daylight brings.

What ails my love; what ails her? She is paling;
    Faint grows her face, and slowly seems to fade!
I cannot clasp her—stretch out unavailing
    My arms across the silence and the shade.

BORDERLAND

Am I waking, am I sleeping?
As the first faint dawn comes creeping
Thro' the pane, I am aware
Of an unseen presence hovering,
Round, above, in the dusky air:
A downy bird, with an odorous wing,
That fans my forehead, and sheds perfume,
As sweet as love, as soft as death,
Drowsy-slow through the summer-gloom.
My heart in some dream-rapture saith,
It is she. Half in a swoon,
I spread my arms in slow delight.—
O prolong, prolong the night,
For the nights are short in June!

At Dawn

In the night I dreamed of you;
    All the place was filled
With your presence; in my heart
    The strife was stilled.

All night I have dreamed of you;
    Now the morn is grey.—
How shall I arise and face
    The empty day?

LAST WORDS

Dead! all's done with!

—R. BROWNING

These blossoms that I bring,
This song that here I sing,
These tears that now I shed,
I give unto the dead.

There is no more to be done,
Nothing beneath the sun,
All the long ages through,
Nothing—by me for you.

The tale is told to the end;
This, ev'n, I may not know—
If we were friend and friend,
If we were foe and foe.

All's done with utterly,
All's done with. Death to me
Was ever Death indeed;
To me no kindly creed

Consolatory was given.
You were of earth, not Heaven. . .
This dreary day, things seem
Vain shadows in a dream,

Or some strange, pictured show;
And mine own tears that flow,
My hidden tears that fall,
The vainest of them all.

JUNE

Last June I saw your face three times;
    Three times I touched your hand;
Now, as before, May month is o'er,
    And June is in the land.

O many Junes shall come and go,
    Flow'r-footed o'er the mead;
O many Junes for me, to whom
    Is length of days decreed.

There shall be sunlight, scent of rose,
    Warm mist of summer rain;
Only this change—I shall not look
    Upon your face again.

A Reminiscence

It is so long gone by, and yet
    How clearly now I see it all!
The glimmer of your cigarette,
    The little chamber, narrow and tall.

Perseus; your picture in its frame;
    (How near they seem and yet how far!)
The blaze of kindled logs; the flame
    Of tulips in a mighty jar.

Florence and spring-time: surely each
    Glad things unto the spirit saith.
Why did you lead me in your speech
    To these dark mysteries of death?

The Sequel to "A Reminiscence"

Not in the street and not in the square,
    The street and square where you went and came;
With shuttered casement your house stands bare,
    Men hush their voice when they speak your name.

I, too, can play at the vain pretence,
    Can feign you dead; while a voice sounds clear
In the inmost depths of my heart: Go hence,
    Go, find your friend who is far from here.

Not here, but somewhere where I can reach!
    Can a man with motion, hearing and sight,
And a thought that answered my thought and speech,
    Be utterly lost and vanished quite?

Whose hand was warm in my hand last week? . . .
    My heart beat fast as I neared the gate—
Was it this I had come to seek,
    "A stone that stared with your name and date;"

A hideous, turfless, fresh-made mound;
    A silence more cold than the wind that blew?
What had I lost, and what had I found?
    My flowers that mocked me fell to the ground—
Then, and then only, my spirit knew.

In the Mile End Road

How like her! But 'tis she herself,
    Comes up the crowded street,
How little did I think, the morn,
    My only love to meet!

Whose else that motion and that mien?
    Whose else that airy tread?
For one strange moment I forgot
    My only love was dead.

Contradictions

Now, even, I cannot think it true,
My friend, that there is no more you.
Almost as soon were no more I,
Which were, of course, absurdity!
Your place is bare, you are not seen,
Your grave, I'm told, is growing green;
And both for you and me, you know,
There's no Above and no Below.
That you are dead must be inferred,
And yet my thought rejects the word.

TWILIGHT

So Mary died last night! Today
    The news has travelled here.
And Robert died at Michaelmas,
    And Walter died last year.

I went at sunset up the lane,
    I lingered by the stile;
I saw the dusky fields that stretched
    Before me many a mile.

I leaned against the stile, and thought
    Of her whose soul had fled.—
I knew that years on years must pass
    Or e'er I should be dead.

In September

The sky is silver-grey; the long
    Slow waves caress the shore.—
On such a day as this I have been glad,
    Who shall be glad no more.

MOODS AND THOUGHTS

I sent my Soul through the Invisible
Some letter of that After-life to spell;
And by and by my Soul returned to me,
And answered, "I Myself am Heaven and Hell."

—OMAR KHAYYÁM

THE OLD HOUSE

In through the porch and up the silent stair;
    Little is changed, I know so well the ways;—
Here, the dead came to meet me; it was there
    The dream was dreamed in unforgotten days.

But who is this that hurries on before,
    A flitting shade the brooding shades among?—
She turned,—I saw her face,—O God, it wore
    The face I used to wear when I was young!

I thought my spirit and my heart were tamed
    To deadness; dead the pangs that agonise.
The old grief springs to choke me,—I am shamed
    Before that little ghost with eager eyes.

O turn away, let her not see, not know!
    How should she bear it, how should understand?
O hasten down the stairway, haste and go,
    And leave her dreaming in the silent land.

LOHENGRIN

Back to the mystic shore beyond the main
The mystic craft has sped, and left no trace.
    Ah, nevermore may she behold his face,
Nor touch his hand, nor hear his voice again!
With hidden front she crouches; all in vain
    The proffered balm. A vessel nears the place;
They bring her young, lost brother; see her strain
    The new-found nursling in a close embrace.

God, we have lost Thee with much questioning.
In vain we seek Thy trace by sea and land,
And in Thine empty fanes where no men sing.
    What shall we do through all the weary days?
    Thus wail we and lament. Our eyes we raise,
And, lo, our Brother with an outstretched hand!

ALMA MATER

A haunted town thou art to me.

—ANDREW LANG

Today in Florence all the air
Is soft with spring, with sunlight fair;
In the tall street gay folks are met;
Duomo and Tower gleam overhead,
Like jewels in the city set,
Fair-hued and many-faceted.
Against the old grey stones are piled
February violets, pale and sweet,
Whose scent of earth in woodland wild
Is wafted up and down the street.
The city's heart is glad; my own
Sits lightly on its bosom's throne.

    *   *   *   *   *

Why is it that I see today,
Imaged as clear as in a dream,
A little city far away,
A churlish sky, a sluggish stream,
Tall clust'ring trees and gardens fair,
Dark birds that circle in the air,
Grey towers and fanes; on either hand,
Stretches of wind-swept meadow-land?

    *   *   *   *   *

Oh, who can sound the human breast?
And this strange truth must be confessed;
That city do I love the best
Wherein my heart was heaviest!

In the Black Forest

I lay beneath the pine trees,
　　And looked aloft, where, through
The dusky, clustered tree-tops,
　　Gleamed rent, gay rifts of blue.

I shut my eyes, and a fancy
　　Fluttered my sense around:
"I lie here dead and buried,
　　And this is churchyard ground.

"I am at rest for ever;
　　Ended the stress and strife."
Straight I fell to and sorrowed
　　For the pitiful past life.

Right wronged, and knowledge wasted;
　　Wise labour spurned for ease;
The sloth and the sin and the failure;
　　Did I grow sad for these?

They had made me sad so often;
　　Not now they made me sad;
My heart was full of sorrow
　　For joy it never had.

Captivity

The lion remembers the forest,
    The lion in chains;
To the bird that is captive a vision
    Of woodland remains.

One strains with his strength at the fetter,
    In impotent rage;
One flutters in flights of a moment,
    And beats at the cage.

If the lion were loosed from the fetter,
    To wander again;
He would seek the wide silence and shadow
    Of his jungle in vain.

He would rage in his fury, destroying;
    Let him rage, let him roam!
Shall he traverse the pitiless mountain,
    Or swim through the foam?

If they opened the cage and the casement,
    And the bird flew away;
He would come back at evening, heartbroken,
    A captive for aye.

Would come if his kindred had spared him,
    Free birds from afar—
There was wrought what is stronger than iron
    In fetter and bar.

I cannot remember my country,
    The land whence I came;
Whence they brought me and chained me and made me
    Nor wild thing nor tame.

This only I know of my country,
    This only repeat:—
It was free as the forest, and sweeter
    Than woodland retreat.

When the chain shall at last be broken,
    The window set wide;
And I step in the largeness and freedom
    Of sunlight outside;

Shall I wander in vain for my country?
    Shall I seek and not find?
Shall I cry for the bars that encage me,
    The fetters that bind?

AMY LEVY

THE TWO TERRORS

Two terrors fright my soul by night and day:
The first is Life, and with her come the years;
A weary, winding train of maidens they,
With forward-fronting eyes, too sad for tears;
Upon whose kindred faces, blank and grey,
The shadow of a kindred woe appears.
Death is the second terror; who shall say
What form beneath the shrouding mantle nears?

Which way she turn, my soul finds no relief,
My smitten soul may not be comforted;
Alternately she swings from grief to grief,
And, poised between them, sways from dread to dread.
For there she dreads because she knows; and here,
Because she knows not, inly faints with fear.

The Promise of Sleep

Put the sweet thoughts from out thy mind,
The dreams from out thy breast;
No joy for thee—but thou shalt find
Thy rest.

All day I could not work for woe,
    I could not work nor rest;
The trouble drove me to and fro,
    Like a leaf on the storm's breast.

Night came and saw my sorrow cease;
    Sleep in the chamber stole;
Peace crept about my limbs, and peace
    Fell on my stormy soul.

And now I think of only this,—
    How I again may woo
The gentle sleep—who promises
    That death is gentle too.

The Last Judgment

With beating heart and lagging feet,
Lord, I approach the Judgment-seat.
All bring hither the fruits of toil,
Measures of wheat and measures of oil;

Gold and jewels and precious wine;
No hands bare like these hands of mine.
The treasure I have nor weighs nor gleams:
Lord, I can bring you only dreams.

In days of spring, when my blood ran high,
I lay in the grass and looked at the sky,
And dreamed that my love lay by my side—
My love was false, and then she died.

All the heat of the summer through,
I dreamed she lived, that her heart was true.
Throughout the hours of the day I slept,
But woke in the night, at times, and wept.

The nights and days, they went and came,
I lay in shadow and dreamed of fame;
And heard men passing the lonely place,
Who marked me not and my hidden face.

My strength waxed faint, my hair grew grey;
Nothing but dreams by night and day.
Some men sicken, with wine and food;
I starved on dreams, and found them good.

*   *   *   *   *

This is the tale I have to tell—
Show the fellow the way to hell.

Felo de Se

With Apologies To Mr. Swinburne

For repose I have sighed and have struggled; have sigh'd and
    have struggled in vain;
I am held in the Circle of Being and caught in the Circle of Pain.
I was wan and weary with life; my sick soul yearned for death;
I was weary of women and war and the sea and the wind's wild breath;
I cull'd sweet poppies and crush'd them, the blood ran rich and red:—
And I cast it in crystal chalice and drank of it till I was dead.
And the mould of the man was mute, pulseless in ev'ry part,
The long limbs lay on the sand with an eagle eating the heart.
Repose for the rotting head and peace for the putrid breast,
But for that which is "I" indeed the gods have decreed no rest;
No rest but an endless aching, a sorrow which grows amain:—
I am caught in the Circle of Being and held in the Circle of Pain.
Bitter indeed is Life, and bitter of Life the breath,
But give me life and its ways and its men, if this be Death.
Wearied I once of the Sun and the voices which clamour'd around:
Give them me back—in the sightless depths there is neither
    light nor sound.
Sick is my soul, and sad and feeble and faint as it felt
When (far, dim day) in the fair flesh-fane of the body it dwelt.
But then I could run to the shore, weeping and weary and weak;
See the waves' blue sheen and feel the breath of the breeze on my
    cheek:
Could wail with the wailing wind; strike sharply the hands in despair;
Could shriek with the shrieking blast, grow frenzied and tear the hair;
Could fight fierce fights with the foe or clutch at a human hand;
And weary could lie at length on the soft, sweet, saffron sand. . .
I have neither a voice nor hands, nor any friend nor a foe;
I am I—just a Pulse of Pain—I am I, that is all I know.
For Life, and the sickness of Life, and Death and desire to die;—
They have passed away like the smoke, here is nothing but Pain and I.

THE LOST FRIEND

The people take the thing of course,
They marvel not to see
This strange, unnatural divorce
Betwixt delight and me.

I know the face of sorrow, and I know
Her voice with all its varied cadences;
Which way she turns and treads; how at her ease
Thinks fit her dreary largess to bestow.

Where sorrow long abides, some be that grow
To hold her dear, but I am not of these;
Joy is my friend, not sorrow; by strange seas,
In some far land we wandered, long ago.

O faith, long tried, that knows no faltering!
O vanished treasure of her hands and face!—
Beloved—to whose memory I cling,
Unmoved within my heart she holds her place.

And never shall I hail that other "friend,"
Who yet shall dog my footsteps to the end.

Cambridge in the Long

Where drowsy sound of college-chimes
    Across the air is blown,
And drowsy fragrance of the limes,
    I lie and dream alone.

A dazzling radiance reigns o'er all—
    O'er gardens densely green,
O'er old grey bridges and the small,
    Slow flood which slides between.

This is the place; it is not strange,
    But known of old and dear.—
What went I forth to seek? The change
    Is mine; why am I here?

Alas, in vain I turned away,
    I fled the town in vain;
The strenuous life of yesterday
    Calleth me back again.

And was it peace I came to seek?
    Yet here, where memories throng,
Ev'n here, I know the past is weak,
    I know the present strong.

This drowsy fragrance, silent heat,
    Suit not my present mind,
Whose eager thought goes out to meet
    The life it left behind.

Spirit with sky to change; such hope,
    An idle one we know;
Unship the oars, make loose the rope,
    Push off the boat and go. . .

Ah, would what binds me could have been
    Thus loosened at a touch!
This pain of living is too keen,
    Of loving, is too much.

To Vernon Lee

On Bellosguardo, when the year was young,
We wandered, seeking for the daffodil
And dark anemone, whose purples fill
The peasant's plot, between the corn-shoots sprung.

Over the grey, low wall the olive flung
Her deeper greyness; far off, hill on hill
Sloped to the sky, which, pearly-pale and still,
Above the large and luminous landscape hung.

A snowy blackthorn flowered beyond my reach;
You broke a branch and gave it to me there;
I found for you a scarlet blossom rare.

Thereby ran on of Art and Life our speech;
And of the gifts the gods had given to each—
Hope unto you, and unto me Despair.

The Old Poet

I will be glad because it is the Spring;
    I will forget the winter in my heart—
Dead hopes and withered promise; and will wring
    A little joy from life ere life depart.

For spendthrift youth with passion-blinded eyes,
    Stays not to see how woods and fields are bright;
He hears the phantom voices call, he flies
    Upon the track of some unknown delight.

To him the tender glory of the May,
    White wonder of the blossom, and the clear,
Soft green of leaves that opened yesterday,
    This only say: Forward, my friend, not here!

They breathe no other messages than this,
    They have no other meaning for his heart;
Unto his troubled sense they tell of bliss,
    Which make, themselves, of bliss the better part.

Yea, joy is near him, tho' he does not know;
    Her unregarded shape is at his side,
Her unheard voice is whispering clear and low,
    Whom, resting never, seeks he far and wide.

So once it was with us, my heart! Today
    We will be glad because the leaves are green,
Because the fields are fair and soft with May,
    Nor think on squandered springtimes that have been.

On the Wye in May

Now is the perfect moment of the year.
    Half naked branches, half a mist of green,
Vivid and delicate the slopes appear;
    The cool, soft air is neither fierce nor keen,

And in the temperate sun we feel no fear;
    Of all the hours which shall be and have been,
It is the briefest as it is most dear,
    It is the dearest as the shortest seen.

O it was best, belovèd, at the first.—
    Our hands met gently, and our meeting sight
Was steady; on our senses scare had burst
    The faint, fresh fragrance of the new delight. . .

I seek that clime, unknown, without a name,
    Where first and best and last shall be the same.

Oh, is it Love?

O is it Love or is it Fame,
    This thing for which I sigh?
Or has it then no earthly name
    For men to call it by?

I know not what can ease my pains,
    Nor what it is I wish;
The passion at my heart-strings strains
    Like a tiger in a leash.

IN THE NOWER

To J. De P.

Deep in the grass outstretched I lie,
    Motionless on the hill;
Above me is a cloudless sky,
    Around me all is still:

There is no breath, no sound, no stir,
    The drowsy peace to break;
I close my tired eyes—it were
    So simple not to wake.

The End of the Day

To B. T.

Dead-tired, dog-tired, as the vivid day
Fails and slackens and fades away.—
The sky that was so blue before
With sudden clouds is shrouded o'er.
Swiftly, stilly the mists uprise,
Till blurred and grey the landscape lies.

     *   *   *   *   *

All day we have plied the oar; all day
Eager and keen have said our say
On life and death, on love and art,
On good or ill at Nature's heart.
Now, grown so tired, we scarce can lift
The lazy oars, but onward drift.
And the silence is only stirred
Here and there by a broken word.

     *   *   *   *   *

O, sweeter far than strain and stress
Is the slow, creeping weariness.
And better far than thought I find
The drowsy blankness of the mind.
More than all joys of soul or sense
Is this divine indifference;
Where grief a shadow grows to be,
And peace a possibility.

ODDS AND ENDS

SONGS FROM *THE NEW PHAON*
(UNPUBLISHED)—

I. A Wall Flower

I lounge in the doorway and languish in vain
While Tom, Dick and Harry are dancing with Jane

My spirit rises to the music's beat;
There is a leaden fiend lurks in my feet!
To move unto your motion, Love, were sweet.

Somewhere, I think, some other where, not here,
In other ages, on another sphere,
I danced with you, and you with me, my dear.

In perfect motion did our bodies sway,
To perfect music that was heard alway;
Woe's me, that am so dull of foot today!

To move unto your motion, Love, were sweet;
My spirit rises to the music's beat—
But, ah, the leaden demon in my feet!

II. The First Extra

A Waltz Song

O sway, and swing, and sway,
   And swing, and sway, and swing!
Ah me, what bliss like unto this,
   Can days and daylight bring?

A rose beneath your feet
   Has fallen from my head;
Its odour rises sweet,
   All crushed it lies, and dead.

O Love is like a rose,
   Fair-hued, of fragrant breath;
A tender flow'r that lives an hour,
   And is most sweet in death.

O swing, and sway, and swing,
   And rise, and sink, and fall!
There is no bliss like unto this,
   This is the best of all.

III. At a Dinner Party

With fruit and flowers the board is deckt,
    The wine and laughter flow;
I'll not complain—could one expect
    So dull a world to know?

You look across the fruit and flowers,
    My glance your glances find.—
It is our secret, only ours,
    Since all the world is blind.

Philosophy

Ere all the world had grown so drear,
When I was young and you were here,
'Mid summer roses in summer weather,
What pleasant times we've had together!

We were not Phyllis, simple-sweet,
And Corydon; we did not meet
By brook or meadow, but among
A Philistine and flippant throng

Which much we scorned; (less rigorous
It had no scorn at all for us!)
How many an eve of sweet July,
Heedless of Mrs. Grundy's eye,

We've scaled the stairway's topmost height,
And sat there talking half the night;
And, gazing on the crowd below,
Thanked Fate and Heaven that made us so;—

To hold the pure delights of brain
Above light loves and sweet champagne.
For, you and I, we did eschew
The egoistic "I" and "you;"

And all our observations ran
On Art and Letters, Life and Man.
Proudly we sat, we two, on high,
Throned in our Objectivity;

Scarce friends, not lovers (each avers),
But sexless, safe Philosophers.

*   *   *   *   *

Dear Friend, you must not deem me light
If, as I lie and muse tonight,
I give a smile and not a sigh
To thoughts of our Philosophy.

A Game of Lawn Tennis

What wonder that I should be dreaming
    Out here in the garden today?
The light through the leaves is streaming,—
        Paulina cries, "Play!"

The birds to each other are calling,
    The freshly-cut grasses smell sweet;
To Teddy's dismay, comes falling
        The ball at my feet.

"Your stroke should be over, not under!"
    "But that's such a difficult way!"
The place is a springtide wonder
        Of lilac and may;

Of lilac, and may, and laburnum,
    Of blossom,— *We'er losing the set!*
"Those volleys of Jenny's,—return them;
    "Stand close to the net!"

      *   *   *   *   *

You are so fond of the Maytime,
    My friend, far away;
Small wonder that I should be dreaming
    Of you in the garden today.

To E.

The mountains in fantastic lines
Sweep, blue-white, to the sky, which shines
Blue as blue gems; athwart the pines
    The lake gleams blue.

We three were here, three years gone by;
Our Poet, with fine-frenzied eye,
You, steeped in learned lore, and I,
    A poet too.

Our Poet brought us books and flowers,
He read us *Faust*; he talked for hours
Philosophy (sad Schopenhauer's),
    Beneath the trees:

And do you mind that sunny day,
When he, as on the sward he lay,
Told of Lassalle who bore away
    The false Louise?

Thrice-favoured bard! to him alone
That green and snug retreat was shown,
Where to the vulgar herd unknown,
    Our pens we plied.

(For, in those distant days, it seems,
We cherished sundry idle dreams,
And with our flowing foolscap reams
    The Fates defied.)

And after, when the day was gone,
And the hushed, silver night came on,
He showed us where the glow-worm shone;—
    We stooped to see.

There, too, by yonder moon we swore
Platonic friendship o'er and o'er;
No folk, we deemed, had been before
                              So wise and free.

        *   *   *   *   *

And do I sigh or smile today?
Dead love or dead ambition, say,
Which mourn we most? Not much we weigh
                              Platonic friends.

On you the sun is shining free;
Our Poet sleeps in Italy,
Beneath an alien sod; on me
                              The cloud descends.

AMY LEVY

A Note About the Author

Amy Levy (1861–1889) was a British poet and novelist. Born in Clapham, London to a Jewish family, she was the second oldest of seven children. Levy developed a passion for literature in her youth, writing a critique of Elizabeth Barrett Browning's *Aurora Leigh* and publishing her first poem by the age of fourteen. After excelling at Brighton and Hove High School, Levy became the first Jewish student at Newnham College, Cambridge, where she studied for several years without completing her degree. Around this time, she befriended such feminist intellectuals as Clementina Black, Ellen Wordsworth Darwin, Eleanor Marx, and Olive Schreiner. As a so-called "New Woman" and lesbian, much of Levy's literary work explores the concerns of nineteenth century feminism. Levy was a romantic partner of Violet Paget, a British storyteller and scholar of Aestheticism who wrote using the pseudonym Vernon Lee. Her first novel, *The Romance of a Shop* (1888), is powerful story of sisterhood and perseverance in the face of poverty and marginalization. Levy is also known for such poetry collections as *A Minor Poet and Other Verse* (1884) and *A London Plane-Tree and Other Verse* (1889). At the age of 27, after a lifetime of depression exacerbated by relationship trouble and her increasing deafness, Levy committed suicide at her parents' home in Endsleigh Gardens.

A Note from the Publisher

Spanning many genres, from non-fiction essays to literature classics to children's books and lyric poetry, Mint Edition books showcase the master works of our time in a modern new package. The text is freshly typeset, is clean and easy to read, and features a new note about the author in each volume. Many books also include exclusive new introductory material. Every book boasts a striking new cover, which makes it as appropriate for collecting as it is for gift giving. Mint Edition books are only printed when a reader orders them, so natural resources are not wasted. We're proud that our books are never manufactured in excess and exist only in the exact quantity they need to be read and enjoyed.

bookfinity™

Discover more of your favorite classics with Bookfinity™.

- Track your reading with custom book lists.
- Get great book recommendations for your personalized Reader Type.
- Add reviews for your favorite books.
- AND MUCH MORE!

Visit **bookfinity.com** and take the fun Reader Type quiz to get started.

Enjoy our classic and modern companion pairings!